BIBLE PROMISES

for you on your

CONFIRMATION

from the
NEW INTERNATIONAL VERSION

inspirio™

Dear Confirmand:

In the past, you may have related to God in a family kind of way. You accepted certain truths about God because your parents and other caring adults accept them. That was a pleasing thing to God, who has instructed you to "honor your father and mother" (Matthew 15:4).

Now that you've completed your Christian confirmation, however, things have changed. You have received the understanding you need to make your beliefs and convictions your own—to grow and mature in your own relationship with God.

Bible Promises for You on Your Confirmation has been designed to help you continue to grow and become established in your personal faith. Use it when you need to remember what the Bible says on a certain topic. Use it to memorize important verses that will strengthen and encourage you. And we've added devotional comments to some topics that we hope you will find helpful as you strive to become the godly person God created you to be.

TABLE OF CONTENTS

If only I may grow firmer,
simpler, quieter, warmer.

Dag Hammarskjöld

ASSURANCE

Faith is being sure of what we hope for
and certain of what we do not see.

Hebrews 11:1

I am convinced that neither death nor
life, neither angels nor demons, neither
the present nor the future, nor any powers, neither height nor depth, nor anything else in all creation, will be able to
separate us from the love of God that is
in Christ Jesus our Lord.

Romans 8:38–39

"Though the mountains be shaken
and the hills be removed,
yet my unfailing love for you will not be shaken
nor my covenant of peace be removed,"
says the Lord, who has compassion on you.

Isaiah 54:10

ASSURANCE

Jesus said, "My sheep listen to my voice;
I know them, and they follow me. I give
them eternal life, and they shall never
perish; no one can snatch them out of my
hand. My Father, who has given them to
me, is greater than all; no one can snatch
them out of my Father's hand."

John 10:27–29

Those who have served well gain an
excellent standing and great assurance
in their faith in Christ Jesus.

1 Timothy 3:13

I am not ashamed, because I know
whom I have believed, and am convinced
that he is able to guard what I have
entrusted to him for that day.

2 Timothy 1:12

ATONEMENT

Since we have confidence to enter the Most Holy Place by the blood of Jesus ... let us draw near to God with a sincere heart in full assurance of faith, having our hearts sprinkled to cleanse us from a guilty conscience and having our bodies washed with pure water.

Hebrews 10:19, 22

This is the confidence we have in approaching God: that if we ask anything according to his will, he hears us. And if we know that he hears us—whatever we ask—we know that we have what we asked of him.

1 John 5:14–15

ATONEMENT

It is God who makes both us and you stand firm in Christ. He anointed us, set his seal of ownership on us, and put his Spirit in our hearts as a deposit, guaranteeing what is to come.

2 Corinthians 1:21–22

Jesus declared, "All that the Father gives me will come to me, and whoever comes to me I will never drive away. For I have come down from heaven not to do my will but to do the will of him who sent me. And this is the will of him who sent me, that I shall lose none of all that he has given me, but raise them up at the last day."

John 6:37–39

ATONEMENT

Christ was sacrificed once to take away the sins of many people; and he will appear a second time, not to bear sin, but to bring salvation to those who are waiting for him.

Hebrews 9:28

When you were dead in your sins and in the uncircumcision of your sinful nature, God made you alive with Christ. He forgave us all our sins, having canceled the written code, with its regulations, that was against us and that stood opposed to us; he took it away, nailing it to the cross.

Colossians 2:13–14

Jesus said, "This is my blood of the covenant, which is poured out for many for the forgiveness of sins."

Matthew 26:28

ATONEMENT

Jesus Christ is the atoning sacrifice for our sins, and not only for ours but also for the sins of the whole world.

1 John 2:2

Since we have now been justified by Christ's blood, how much more shall we be saved from God's wrath through him!

Romans 5:9

This is love: not that we loved God, but that he loved us and sent his Son as an atoning sacrifice for our sins.

1 John 4:10

God was pleased to have all his fullness dwell in him, and through him to reconcile to himself all things, whether things on earth or things in heaven, by making peace through his blood, shed on the cross.

Colossians 1:19–20

BAPTISM

All of us who were baptized into Christ Jesus were baptized into his death. We were therefore buried with him through baptism into death in order that, just as Christ was raised from the dead through the glory of the Father, we too may live a new life.

Romans 6:3–4

You were also circumcised . . . not with a circumcision done by the hands of men but with the circumcision done by Christ, having been buried with him in baptism and raised with him through your faith in the power of God, who raised him from the dead.

Colossians 2:11–12

BAPTISM

John answered them all, "I baptize you with water. But one more powerful than I will come, the thongs of whose sandals I am not worthy to untie. He will baptize you with the Holy Spirit and with fire."

Luke 3:16

There is one body and one Spirit—just as you were called to one hope when you were called—one Lord, one faith, one baptism; one God and Father of all, who is over all and through all and in all.

Ephesians 4:4–6

Water symbolizes baptism that now saves you also—not the removal of dirt from the body but the pledge of a good conscience toward God. It saves you by the resurrection of Jesus Christ.

1 Peter 3:21

BELIEF

Jesus said, "God so loved the world that he gave his one and only Son, that whoever believes in him shall not perish but have eternal life."

John 3:16

If you confess with your mouth, "Jesus is Lord," and believe in your heart that God raised him from the dead, you will be saved. For it is with your heart that you believe and are justified, and it is with your mouth that you confess and are saved.

Romans 10:9–10

Jesus said, "I tell you the truth, he who believes has everlasting life."

John 6:47

They replied, "Believe in the Lord Jesus, and you will be saved—you and your household."

Acts 16:31

BELIEF

Jesus said to her, "I am the resurrection and the life. He who believes in me will live, even though he dies; and whoever lives and believes in me will never die. Do you believe this?"

John 11:25–26

Jesus said, "Whoever believes in God's Son is not condemned."

John 3:18

All the prophets testify about Jesus Christ that everyone who believes in him receives forgiveness of sins through his name.

Acts 10:43

To all who received him, to those who believed in his name, he gave the right to become children of God.

John 1:12

Jesus told him, "Because you have seen me, you have believed; blessed are those who have not seen and yet have believed."

John 20:29

BIBLE STUDY

If you pay attention to these laws and are
careful to follow them, then the LORD
your God will keep his covenant of love
with you, as he swore to your forefathers.

Deuteronomy 7:12

Jesus answered, "It is written: 'Man does
not live on bread alone, but on every
word that comes from the mouth of God.'"

Matthew 4:4

The law of the LORD is perfect,
reviving the soul.
The statutes of the LORD are trustworthy,
making wise the simple.

Psalm 19:7

When your words came, I ate them;
they were my joy and my heart's delight.

Jeremiah 15:16

Great peace have they who love your law,
and nothing can make them stumble.

Psalm 119:165

BIBLE STUDY

Jesus replied, "Blessed ... are those who hear the word of God and obey it."

Luke 11:28

All Scripture is God-breathed and is useful for teaching, rebuking, correcting and training in righteousness, so that the man of God may be thoroughly equipped for every good work.

2 Timothy 3:16–17

Everything that was written in the past was written to teach us, so that through endurance and the encouragement of the Scriptures we might have hope.

Romans 15:4

Do not let this Book of the Law depart from your mouth; meditate on it day and night, so that you may be careful to do everything written in it. Then you will be prosperous and successful.

Joshua 1:8

BIBLE STUDY

The word of God is living and active. Sharper than any double-edged sword, it penetrates even to dividing soul and spirit, joints and marrow; it judges the thoughts and attitudes of the heart.

Hebrews 4:12

We have the word of the prophets made more certain, and you will do well to pay attention to it, as to a light shining in a dark place, until the day dawns and the morning star rises in your hearts.

2 Peter 1:19

Jesus said to them, "Others, like seed sown on good soil, hear the word, accept it, and produce a crop—thirty, sixty or even a hundred times what was sown."

Mark 4:20

BIBLE STUDY

The unfolding of your words gives light,
O God;
it gives understanding to the simple.

Psalm 119:130

Do your best to present yourself to God
as one approved, a workman who does
not need to be ashamed and who cor-
rectly handles the word of truth.

2 Timothy 2:15

The man who looks intently into the perfect law that gives freedom, and continues to do this, not forgetting what he has
heard, but doing it—he will be blessed in
what he does.

James 1:25

I have hidden your word in my heart
that I might not sin against you.

Psalm 119:11

BLESSINGS

Jesus said,
"Blessed are the poor in spirit,
*   for theirs is the kingdom of heaven."*

Matthew 5:3

Blessed is the man
*   who does not walk in the counsel of the*
*   wicked*
or stand in the way of sinners
*   or sit in the seat of mockers.*
But his delight is in the law of the LORD,
*   and on his law he meditates day and*
*   night.*

Psalm 1:1–2

Blessed is the man who trusts in the LORD,
*   whose confidence is in him.*

Jeremiah 17:7

Praise be to the God and Father of our
Lord Jesus Christ, who has blessed us in
the heavenly realms with every spiritual
blessing in Christ.

Ephesians 1:3

BLESSINGS

Blessed are those you choose
    and bring near to live in your courts!
We are filled with the good things of
        your house,
    of your holy temple.

Psalm 65:4

From the fullness of his grace we have
all received one blessing after another.

John 1:16

Praise the LORD, *O my soul,*
    and forget not all his benefits—
who forgives all your sins
    and heals all your diseases.

Psalm 103:2–3

There is no difference between Jew and
Gentile—the same Lord is Lord of all and
richly blesses all who call on him, for,
"Everyone who calls on the name of the
Lord will be saved."

Romans 10:12–13

BLESSINGS

Every good and perfect gift is from above, coming down from the Father of the heavenly lights, who does not change like shifting shadows.

James 1:17

You have made known to me the path of life;
     you will fill me with joy in your presence,
     with eternal pleasures at your right hand.

Psalm 16:11

"I will satisfy the priests with abundance,
     and my people will be filled with my
          bounty,"

declares the LORD.

Jeremiah 31:14

How great is your goodness,
     which you have stored up for those who
          fear you,
which you bestow in the sight of men
     on those who take refuge in you.

Psalm 31:19

BLESSINGS

"Bring the whole tithe into the store-house, that there may be food in my house. Test me in this," says the LORD Almighty, "and see if I will not throw open the floodgates of heaven and pour out so much blessing that you will not have room enough for it."

Malachi 3:10

The LORD had said to Abram,
*"I will make you into a great nation
    and I will bless you;
I will make your name great,
    and you will be a blessing.
I will bless those who bless you,
    and whoever curses you I will curse;
and all peoples on earth
    will be blessed through you."*

Genesis 12:1-3

BLOOD OF JESUS

Jesus took the cup, gave thanks and offered it to them, saying, "Drink from it, all of you. This is my blood of the covenant, which is poured out for many for the forgiveness of sins."

Matthew 26:27–28

God was pleased to have all his fullness dwell in him, and through him to reconcile to himself all things, whether things on earth or things in heaven, by making peace through his blood, shed on the cross.

Colossians 1:19–20

If we walk in the light, as he is in the light, we have fellowship with one another, and the blood of Jesus, his Son, purifies us from all sin.

1 John 1:7

BLOOD OF JESUS

God has reconciled you by Christ's physical body through death to present you holy in his sight, without blemish and free from accusation.

Colossians 1:22

In Christ Jesus you who once were far away have been brought near through the blood of Christ.

Ephesians 2:13

Since we have now been justified by Jesus' blood, how much more shall we be saved from God's wrath through him!

Romans 5:9

It was not with perishable things such as silver or gold that you were redeemed from the empty way of life handed down to you from your forefathers, but with the precious blood of Christ, a lamb without blemish or defect.

1 Peter 1:18–19

BLOOD OF JESUS

To him who loves us and has freed us from our sins by his blood, and has made us to be a kingdom and priests to serve his God and Father—to him be glory and power for ever and ever!

Revelation 1:5–6

Jesus said to them, "I tell you the truth, unless you eat the flesh of the Son of Man and drink his blood, you have no life in you. Whoever eats my flesh and drinks my blood has eternal life, and I will raise him up at the last day."

John 6:53–54

In Jesus we have redemption through his blood, the forgiveness of sins, in accordance with the riches of God's grace that he lavished on us with all wisdom and understanding.

Ephesians 1:7–8

BLOOD OF JESUS

All have sinned and fall short of the glory of God, and are justified freely by his grace through the redemption that came by Christ Jesus. God presented him as a sacrifice of atonement, through faith in his blood. He did this to demonstrate his justice, because in his forbearance he had left the sins committed beforehand unpunished—he did it to demonstrate his justice at the present time, so as to be just and the one who justifies those who have faith in Jesus.

Romans 3:23–26

BOLDNESS

The righteous are as bold as a lion.

Proverbs 28:1

We say with confidence,
"The Lord is my helper; I will not be afraid.
What can man do to me?"

Hebrews 13:6

Because the Sovereign LORD *helps me,*
I will not be disgraced.
Therefore have I set my face like flint,
and I know I will not be put to shame.

Isaiah 50:7

Those who have served well gain an excellent standing and great assurance in their faith in Christ Jesus.

1 Timothy 3:13

BOLDNESS

Have I not commanded you? Be strong
and courageous. Do not be terrified; do
not be discouraged, for the LORD your
God will be with you wherever you go.

Joshua 1:9

As for me, I am filled with power,
with the Spirit of the LORD,
and with justice and might,
to declare to Jacob his transgression,
to Israel his sin.

Micah 3:8

When I called, you answered me;
you made me bold and stouthearted.

Psalm 138:3

Let us then approach the throne of
grace with confidence, so that we may
receive mercy and find grace to help us
in our time of need.

Hebrews 4:16

CHARACTER

Jesus said,
"Blessed are those who hunger and thirst
for righteousness,
for they will be filled."

Matthew 5:6

The LORD does not look at the things
man looks at. Man looks at the outward
appearance, but the LORD looks at the
heart.

1 Samuel 16:7

A man's ways are in full view of the LORD,
and he examines all his paths.

Proverbs 5:21

The highway of the upright avoids evil;
he who guards his way guards his life.

Proverbs 16:17

We know that suffering produces perseverance; perseverance, character; and
character, hope. And hope does not dis-
appoint us, because God has poured out
his love into our hearts by the Holy
Spirit, whom he has given us.

Romans 5:3–5

CHARACTER

The noble man makes noble plans,
*   and by noble deeds he stands.*

Isaiah 32:8

Blessed are they whose ways are blameless,
*   who walk according to the law of the LORD.*

Psalm 119:1

Blessed are the merciful,
*   for they will be shown mercy.*

Matthew 5:7

A good name is more desirable than great riches;
*   to be esteemed is better than silver or gold.*

Proverbs 22:1

Let us hold unswervingly to the hope we profess, for God who promised is faithful.

Hebrews 10:23

Jesus said, "When you pray, go into your room, close the door and pray to your Father, who is unseen. Then your Father, who sees what is done in secret, will reward you."

Matthew 6:6

CHARITY

Blessed is he who has regard for the weak;
　the LORD delivers him in times of trouble.
The LORD will protect him and preserve his life.

Psalm 41:1–2

He who is kind to the poor lends to the LORD,
　and he will reward him for what he has done.

Proverbs 19:17

Jesus said, "I tell you the truth, whatever
you did for one of the least of these
brothers of mine, you did for me."

Matthew 25:40

A generous man will himself be blessed,
　for he shares his food with the poor.

Proverbs 22:9

CHARITY

Jesus said, "If anyone gives even a cup of cold water to one of these little ones because he is my disciple, I tell you the truth, he will certainly not lose his reward."

Matthew 10:42

Jesus said, "When you give a banquet, invite the poor, the crippled, the lame, the blind, and you will be blessed. Although they cannot repay you, you will be repaid at the resurrection of the righteous."

Luke 14:13–14

Each man should give what he has decided in his heart to give, not reluctantly or under compulsion, for God loves a cheerful giver.

2 Corinthians 9:7

CHARITY

Blessed is he who is kind to the needy.

Proverbs 14:21

A generous man will prosper;
*   he who refreshes others will himself be*
*   refreshed.*

Proverbs 11:25

Jesus said, "When you give to the needy,
do not let your left hand know what
your right hand is doing, so that your
giving may be in secret. Then your
Father, who sees what is done in secret,
will reward you."

Matthew 6:3–4

He who gives to the poor will lack nothing.

Proverbs 28:27

Jesus said, "Give to everyone who asks
you, and if anyone takes what belongs to
you, do not demand it back."

Luke 6:30

CHARITY

Jesus said, "Give, and it will be given to you. A good measure, pressed down, shaken together and running over, will be poured into your lap. For with the measure you use, it will be measured to you."

Luke 6:38

If there is a poor man among your brothers ... give generously to him and do so without a grudging heart; then because of this the LORD your God will bless you in all your work and in everything you put your hand to.

Deuteronomy 15:7, 10

Jesus said, "If you then, though you are evil, know how to give good gifts to your children, how much more will your Father in heaven give the Holy Spirit to those who ask him!"

Luke 11:13

CHRIST'S RETURN

Jesus said, "In my Father's house are many rooms; if it were not so, I would have told you. I am going there to prepare a place for you. And if I go and prepare a place for you, I will come back and take you to be with me that you also may be where I am."

John 14:2–3

"Men of Galilee," the two men dressed in white said, "why do you stand here looking into the sky? This same Jesus, who has been taken from you into heaven, will come back in the same way you have seen him go into heaven."

Acts 1:11

Look, he is coming with the clouds,
and every eye will see him.

Revelation 1:7

CHRIST'S RETURN

The day of the Lord will come like a thief. The heavens will disappear with a roar; the elements will be destroyed by fire, and the earth and everything in it will be laid bare.

2 Peter 3:10

Jesus said, "You also must be ready, because the Son of Man will come at an hour when you do not expect him."

Luke 12:40

Jesus said, "Behold, I am coming soon! My reward is with me, and I will give to everyone according to what he has done."

Revelation 22:12

Jesus said, "This gospel of the kingdom will be preached in the whole world as a testimony to all nations, and then the end will come."

Matthew 24:14

CHURCH

The body is a unit, though it is made up of many parts; and though all its parts are many, they form one body. So it is with Christ. For we were all baptized by one Spirit into one body—whether Jews or Greeks, slave or free—and we were all given the one Spirit to drink.

1 Corinthians 12:12-13

You are a chosen people, a royal priesthood, a holy nation, a people belonging to God, that you may declare the praises of him who called you out of darkness into his wonderful light.

1 Peter 2:9

God's household ... is the church of the living God, the pillar and foundation of the truth.

1 Timothy 3:15

CHURCH

You are the body of Christ, and each one of you is a part of it. And in the church God has appointed first of all apostles, second prophets, third teachers, then workers of miracles, also those having gifts of healing, those able to help others, those with gifts of administration, and those speaking in different kinds of tongues.

1 Corinthians 12:27-28

Christ is the head of the body, the church; he is the beginning and the firstborn from among the dead, so that in everything he might have the supremacy.

Colossians 1:18

Let us not give up meeting together, as some are in the habit of doing, but let us encourage one another—and all the more as you see the Day approaching.

Hebrews 10:25

CHURCH

Obey your leaders and submit to their authority. They keep watch over you as men who must give an account. Obey them so that their work will be a joy, not a burden, for that would be of no advantage to you.

Hebrews 13:17

Jesus replied, "Blessed are you, Simon son of Jonah, for this was not revealed to you by man, but by my Father in heaven. And I tell you that you are Peter, and on this rock I will build my church, and the gates of Hades will not overcome it."

Matthew 16:17–18

CHURCH

Just as each of us has one body with many members, and these members do not all have the same function, so in Christ we who are many form one body, and each member belongs to all the others. We have different gifts, according to the grace given us. If a man's gift is prophesying, let him use it in proportion to his faith.

Romans 12:4–6

You are no longer foreigners and aliens, but fellow citizens with God's people and members of God's household, built on the foundation of the apostles and prophets, with Christ Jesus himself as the chief cornerstone. In him the whole building is joined together and rises to become a holy temple in the Lord.

Ephesians 2:19–21

COMMITMENT

Commit your way to the LORD;
   trust in him and he will do this.

Psalm 37:5

Commit to the LORD whatever you do,
   and your plans will succeed.

Proverbs 16:3

Your hearts must be fully committed to
the LORD our God, to live by his decrees
and obey his commands, as at this time.

1 Kings 8:61

From everlasting to everlasting
   the LORD's love is with those who fear him,
   and his righteousness with their children's
      children—
with those who keep his covenant
   and remember to obey his precepts.

Psalm 103:17–18

COMMITMENT

When a man makes a vow to the Lord or takes an oath to obligate himself by a pledge, he must not break his word but must do everything he said.

Numbers 30:2

When you make a vow to God, do not delay in fulfilling it. He has no pleasure in fools; fulfill your vow.

Ecclesiastes 5:4

The eyes of the Lord range throughout the earth to strengthen those whose hearts are fully committed to him.

2 Chronicles 16:9

COMMUNICATION

Confess your sins to each other and pray
for each other so that you may be healed.

James 5:16

He who guards his lips guards his life.

Proverbs 13:3

From the fruit of his mouth a man's stomach
   is filled;
   with the harvest from his lips he is satisfied.

Proverbs 18:20

The mouth of the righteous man utters wisdom,
   and his tongue speaks what is just.
The law of his God is in his heart;
   his feet do not slip.

Psalm 37:30–31

He who holds his tongue is wise.
   The tongue of the righteous is choice silver.

Proverbs 10:19–20

COMMUNICATION

We will no longer be infants, tossed back and forth by the waves, and blown here and there by every wind of teaching and by the cunning and craftiness of men in their deceitful scheming. Instead, speaking the truth in love, we will in all things grow up into him who is the Head, that is, Christ.

Ephesians 4:14-15

May the words of my mouth and
*   the meditation of my heart*
be pleasing in your sight,
*   O LORD.*

Psalm 19:14

Always be prepared to give an answer to everyone who asks you to give the reason for the hope that you have. But do this with gentleness and respect.

1 Peter 3:15

COMMUNICATION

Set a guard over my mouth, O LORD;
   keep watch over the door of my lips.

Psalm 141:3

If anyone is never at fault in what he
says, he is a perfect man, able to keep
his whole body in check.

James 3:2

From the fruit of his lips a man enjoys
     good things.

Proverbs 13:2

A wise man's heart guides his mouth,
   and his lips promote instruction.
Pleasant words are a honeycomb,
   sweet to the soul and healing to the bones.

Proverbs 16:23–24

A gentle answer turns away wrath,
   but a harsh word stirs up anger.
The tongue of the wise commends knowledge.

Proverbs 15:1–2

COMMUNICATION

The tongue that brings healing is a tree of life.

Proverbs 15:4

Let your conversation be always full of grace, seasoned with salt, so that you may know how to answer everyone.

Colossians 4:6

*The Sovereign LORD has given me an
    instructed tongue,
  to know the word that sustains the weary.*

Isaiah 50:4

If anyone speaks, he should do it as one speaking the very words of God.

1 Peter 4:11

*The quiet words of the wise are more to be
    heeded
  than the shouts of a ruler of fools.*

Ecclesiastes 9:17

*He who guards his mouth and his tongue
  keeps himself from calamity.*

Proverbs 21:23

COMMUNION

Is not the cup of thanksgiving for which we give thanks a participation in the blood of Christ? And is not the bread that we break a participation in the body of Christ? Because there is one loaf, we, who are many, are one body, for we all partake of the one loaf.

1 Corinthians 10:16–17

Jesus took the cup, gave thanks and offered it to them, saying, "Drink from it, all of you. This is my blood of the covenant, which is poured out for many for the forgiveness of sins. I tell you, I will not drink of this fruit of the vine from now on until that day when I drink it anew with you in my Father's kingdom."

Matthew 26:27–29

COMMUNION

When the hour came, Jesus and his
apostles reclined at the table. And he said
to them, "I have eagerly desired to eat
this Passover with you before I suffer. For
I tell you, I will not eat it again until it
finds fulfillment in the kingdom of God."

Luke 22:14–16

Jesus said to them, "I tell you the truth,
unless you eat the flesh of the Son of
Man and drink his blood, you have no
life in you. Whoever eats my flesh and
drinks my blood has eternal life, and I
will raise him up at the last day."

John 6:53 54

Jesus took bread, gave thanks and broke
it, and gave it to his apostles, saying,
"This is my body given for you; do this
in remembrance of me."

Luke 22:19

COMPASSION

Be kind and compassionate to one another, forgiving each other, just as in Christ God forgave you. Be imitators of God, therefore, as dearly loved children and live a life of love, just as Christ loved us and gave himself up for us as a fragrant offering and sacrifice to God

Ephesians 4:32—5:1–2

Let your compassion come to me that I may live,
for your law is my delight.

Psalm 119: 77

The LORD longs to be gracious to you;
he rises to show you compassion.
For the LORD is a God of justice.
Blessed are all who wait for him!

Isaiah 30:18

COMPASSION

You, O Lord, are a compassionate and
    gracious God,
  slow to anger, abounding in love and
    faithfulness.

                    Psalm 86:15

The Lord is good to all;
  he has compassion on all he has made.

                    Psalm 145:9

"Though the mountains be shaken
  and the hills be removed,
yet my unfailing love for you will not
    be shaken
    nor my covenant of peace be removed,"
says the LORD, who has compassion on you.

                    Isaiah 54:10

I will betroth you to me forever;
  I will betroth you in righteousness and justice,
  in love and compassion.

                    Hosea 2:19

CONTENTMENT

Keep your lives free from the love of money and be content with what you have, because God has said,
"Never will I leave you;
never will I forsake you."

Hebrews 13:5

Better a little with righteousness
than much gain with injustice.

Proverbs 16:8

I am not saying this because I am in need, for I have learned to be content whatever the circumstances. I know what it is to be in need, and I know what it is to have plenty I have learned the secret of being content in any and every situation, whether well fed or hungry, whether living in plenty or in want.

Philippians 4:11–12

If we have food and clothing, we will be content with that.

1 Timothy 6:8

CONTENTMENT

Each one should retain the place in life that the Lord assigned to him and to which God has called him.

1 Corinthians 7:17

Godliness with contentment is great gain.

1 Timothy 6:6

Better the little that the righteous have
*   than the wealth of many wicked;*
for the power of the wicked will be broken,
*   but the LORD upholds the righteous.*

Psalm 37:16–17

The fear of the LORD leads to life;
*   Then one rests content, untouched*
*   by trouble.*

Proverbs 19:23

Better one handful with tranquility
*   than two handfuls with toil*
*   and chasing after the wind.*

Ecclesiastes 4:6

CREATION

In the beginning God created the heavens and the earth. Now the earth was formless and empty, darkness was over the surface of the deep, and the Spirit of God was hovering over the waters.

Genesis 1:1–2

Nothing in all creation is hidden from God's sight. Everything is uncovered and laid bare before the eyes of him to whom we must give account.

Hebrews 4:13

Since the creation of the world God's invisible qualities—his eternal power and divine nature—have been clearly seen, being understood from what has been made, so that men are without excuse.

Romans 1:20

CREATION

Praise be to the God and Father of our Lord Jesus Christ, who has blessed us in the heavenly realms with every spiritual blessing in Christ. For he chose us in him before the creation of the world to be holy and blameless in his sight.

Ephesians 1:3-4

Christ is the image of the invisible God, the firstborn over all creation. For by him all things were created: things in heaven and on earth, visible and invisible, whether thrones or powers or rulers or authorities; all things were created by him and for him.

Colossians 1:15-16

DECISION MAKING

This is what the LORD Almighty says:
"Give careful thought to your ways."

Haggai 1:5

Preserve sound judgment and discernment,
    do not let them out of your sight;
they will be life for you,
    an ornament to grace your neck.
Then you will go on your way in safety,
    and your foot will not stumble;
when you lie down, you will not be afraid;
    when you lie down, your sleep will be sweet.

Proverbs 3:21–24

Commit your way to the LORD;
    trust in him and he will do this:
He will make your righteousness
        shine like the dawn,
    the justice of your cause like the
        noonday sun.

Psalm 37:5–6

DECISION MAKING

Who has known the mind of the Lord
that he may instruct him? But we have
the mind of Christ.

1 Corinthians 2:16

If any of you lacks wisdom, he should ask
God, who gives generously to all without
finding fault, and it will be given to him.

James 1:5

Trust in the LORD with all your heart
and lean not on your own understanding;
in all your ways acknowledge him,
and he will make your paths straight.

Proverbs 3:5–6

Jesus said, "I will ask the Father, and he
will give you another Counselor to be
with you forever—the Spirit of truth."

John 14:16–17

DEFENDING THE WEAK

Learn to do right!
Seek justice,
   encourage the oppressed.
Defend the cause of the fatherless,
   plead the case of the widow.

Isaiah 1:17

Jesus said, "If anyone gives even a cup of cold water to one of these little ones because he is my disciple, I tell you the truth, he will certainly not lose his reward."

Matthew 10:42

We who are strong ought to bear with the failings of the weak and not to please ourselves.

Romans 15:1

We urge you, warn those who are idle, encourage the timid, help the weak, be patient with everyone.

1 Thessalonians 5:14

DEFENDING THE WEAK

The righteous care about justice for the poor.

Proverbs 29:7

Jesus said, "I was hungry and you gave me something to eat, I was thirsty and you gave me something to drink, I was a stranger and you invited me in, I needed clothes and you clothed me, I was sick and you looked after me, I was in prison and you came to visit me."

Matthew 25:35–36

Speak up for those who cannot speak for themselves,
  for the rights of all who are destitute.
Speak up and judge fairly;
  defend the rights of the poor and needy.

Proverbs 31:8–9

DEFENDING THE WEAK

Each of you should look not only to your own interests, but also to the interests of others.

Philippians 2:4

He has showed you, O man, what is good.
    And what does the LORD require of you?
To act justly and to love mercy
    and to walk humbly with your God.

Micah 6:8

Defend the cause of the weak and fatherless;
    maintain the rights of the poor and oppressed.
Rescue the weak and needy;
    deliver them from the hand of the wicked.

Psalm 82:3–4

The LORD gives strength to the weary
    and increases the power of the weak.

Isaiah 40:29

DEFENDING THE WEAK

You hear, O Lord, the desire of the afflicted—
*   you encourage them, and you listen to*
*   their cry,*
defending the fatherless and the oppressed,
*   in order that man, who is of the earth,*
*   may terrify no more.*

Psalm 10:17–18

"Because of the oppression of the weak
*   and the groaning of the needy,*
I will now arise," says the Lord.
*   "I will protect them from those who malign*
*   them."*

Psalm 12:5

The Lord says, "I will search for the lost
and bring back the strays. I will bind up
the injured and strengthen the weak."

Ezekiel 34:16

DEVOTION TO GOD

Jesus replied: "Love the Lord your God with all your heart and with all your soul and with all your mind. This is the first and greatest commandment."

Matthew 22:37–38

Acknowledge the God of your father, and serve him with wholehearted devotion and with a willing mind, for the LORD searches every heart and understands every motive behind the thoughts. If you seek him, he will be found by you; but if you forsake him, he will reject you forever.

1 Chronicles 28:9

Jesus said, "No one can serve two masters. Either he will hate the one and love the other, or he will be devoted to the one and despise the other. You cannot serve both God and Money."

Matthew 6:24

DEVOTION TO GOD

If you devote your heart to him
and stretch out your hands to him,
then you will lift up your face without shame;
you will stand firm and without fear.
You will be secure, because there is hope;
you will look about you and take your rest
in safety.

Job 11:13, 15, 18

My eyes are fixed on you, O Sovereign LORD;
in you I take refuge.

Psalm 141:8

Love the LORD your God with all your
heart and with all your soul and with all
your strength.

Deuteronomy 6:5

Guard my life, for I am devoted to you.
You are my God; save your servant
who trusts in you.

Psalm 86:2

DISCERNMENT

"Give your servant a discerning heart to govern your people and to distinguish between right and wrong. For who is able to govern this great people of yours?" The Lord was pleased that Solomon had asked for this.

1 Kings 3:9-10

Wisdom is found on the lips of the discerning,
but a rod is for the back of him who lacks judgment.

Proverbs 10:13

Whoever obeys his command will come to no harm,
and the wise heart will know the proper time and procedure.

Ecclesiastes 8:5

If any of you lacks wisdom, he should ask God, who gives generously to all without finding fault, and it will be given to him.

James 1:5

DISCERNMENT

Folly delights a man who lacks judgment,
but a man of understanding keeps a straight
course.

Proverbs 15:21

Jesus said, "All that belongs to the Father
is mine. That is why I said the Spirit will
take from what is mine and make it
known to you."

John 16:15

Endure hardship with us like a good sol-
dier of Christ Jesus. Reflect on what I am
saying, for the Lord will give you insight
into all this.

2 Timothy 2:3, 7

We are from God, and whoever knows
God listens to us; but whoever is not
from God does not listen to us. This is
how we recognize the Spirit of truth and
the spirit of falsehood.

1 John 4:6

DISCERNMENT

Test everything. Hold on to the good.
Avoid every kind of evil.

1 Thessalonians 5:21–22

We know that we have come to know
him if we obey his commands.

1 John 2:3

A rich man may be wise in his own eyes,
   but a poor man who has discernment sees
      through him.

Proverbs 28:11

The man without the Spirit does not
accept the things that come from the
Spirit of God, for they are foolishness to
him, and he cannot understand them,
because they are spiritually discerned.
The spiritual man makes judgments
about all things, but he himself is not
subject to any man's judgment:
"For who has known the mind of the Lord
   that he may instruct him?"
But we have the mind of Christ.

1 Corinthians 2:14–16

DISCERNMENT

Preserve sound judgment and discernment,
do not let them out of your sight;
they will be life for you,
an ornament to grace your neck.

Proverbs 3:21–22

This is my prayer: that your love may abound more and more in knowledge and depth of insight, so that you may be able to discern what is best and may be pure and blameless until the day of Christ.

Philippians 1:9–10

I am your servant; give me discernment
that I may understand your statutes.

Psalm 119:125

DISCIPLESHIP

Jesus said, "Whoever serves me must follow me; and where I am, my servant also will be. My Father will honor the one who serves me."

John 12:26

Jesus said to his disciples, "If anyone would come after me, he must deny himself and take up his cross and follow me. For whoever wants to save his life will lose it, but whoever loses his life for me will find it."

Matthew 16:24-25

When Jesus spoke again to the people, he said, "I am the light of the world. Whoever follows me will never walk in darkness, but will have the light of life."

John 8:12

To the Jews who had believed him, Jesus said, "If you hold to my teaching, you are really my disciples."

John 8:31

DISCIPLESHIP

Jesus said, "Whoever has my commands and obeys them, he is the one who loves me. He who loves me will be loved by my Father, and I too will love him and show myself to him."

John 14:21

In the presence of God and of Christ Jesus, who will judge the living and the dead, and in view of his appearing and his kingdom, I give you this charge: Preach the Word; be prepared in season and out of season; correct, rebuke and encourage—with great patience and careful instruction.

2 Timothy 4:1–2

Jesus said, "This is to my Father's glory, that you bear much fruit, showing yourselves to be my disciples."

John 15:8

ETERNAL LIFE

Jesus said, "This is eternal life: that they may know you the only true God, and Jesus Christ, whom you have sent."

John 17:3

The wages of sin is death, but the gift of God is eternal life in Christ Jesus our Lord.

Romans 6:23

Jesus said, "God so loved the world that he gave his one and only Son, that whoever believes in him shall not perish but have eternal life."

John 3:16

This is the testimony: God has given us eternal life, and this life is in his Son. He who has the Son has life; he who does not have the Son of God does not have life.

1 John 5:11–12

John the Baptist said, "Whoever believes in the Son has eternal life."

John 3:36

ETERNAL LIFE

Jesus said to her, "I am the resurrection and the life. He who believes in me will live, even though he dies; and whoever lives and believes in me will never die. Do you believe this?"

John 11:25–26

Having been justified by his grace, we might become heirs having the hope of eternal life.

Titus 3:7

Jesus said, "My sheep listen to my voice; I know them, and they follow me. I give them eternal life, and they shall never perish; no one can snatch them out of my hand. My Father, who has given them to me, is greater than all; no one can snatch them out of my Father's hand."

John 10:27–29

EVANGELISM

Give thanks to the Lord, call on his name;
make known among the nations what he
has done.
Sing to him, sing praise to him;
tell of all his wonderful acts.

1 Chronicles 16:8–9

Jesus said, "Go and make disciples of all nations, baptizing them in the name of the Father and of the Son and of the Holy Spirit, and teaching them to obey everything I have commanded you. And surely I am with you always, to the very end of the age."

Matthew 28:19–20

In your hearts set apart Christ as Lord. Always be prepared to give an answer to everyone who asks you to give the reason for the hope that you have. But do this with gentleness and respect.

1 Peter 3:15

EVANGELISM

Jesus said, "No one lights a lamp and hides it in a jar or puts it under a bed. Instead, he puts it on a stand, so that those who come in can see the light."

Luke 8:16

Jesus said, "Whoever acknowledges me before men, I will also acknowledge him before my Father in heaven."

Matthew 10:32

Jesus said, "Peace be with you! As the Father has sent me, I am sending you."

John 20:21

I pray that you may be active in sharing your faith, so that you will have a full understanding of every good thing we have in Christ.

Philemon 1:6

The apostle Paul said, "I am not ashamed of the gospel, because it is the power of God for the salvation of every one who believes."

Romans 1:16

FAITH

Blessed is the man
*who makes the L*ORD *his trust,*
who does not look to the proud,
to those who turn aside to false gods.

Psalm 40:4

*Blessed is the man who fears the L*ORD*,*
who finds great delight in his commands.
He will have no fear of bad news;
*his heart is steadfast, trusting in the L*ORD*.*
His heart is secure, he will have no fear;
in the end he will look in triumph on his foes.

Psalm 112:1, 7–8

In addition to all this, take up the shield
of faith, with which you can extinguish
all the flaming arrows of the evil one.

Ephesians 6:16

FAITH

Jesus replied, "I tell you the truth, if you have faith and do not doubt, not only can you do what was done to the fig tree, but also you can say to this mountain, 'Go, throw yourself into the sea,' and it will be done."

Matthew 21:21

Pursue righteousness, godliness, faith, love, endurance and gentleness.

1 Timothy 6:11

Some trust in chariots and some in horses,
but we trust in the name of the Lord our God.

Psalm 20:7

Through Christ you believe in God, who raised him from the dead and glorified him, and so your faith and hope are in God.

1 Peter 1:21

FAITH

May your unfailing love rest upon us, O LORD,
*   even as we put our hope in you.*

Psalm 33:22

What does the Scripture say? "Abraham believed God, and it was credited to him as righteousness."

Romans 4:3

Jesus said, "I tell you the truth, anyone who has faith in me will do what I have been doing. He will do even greater things than these, because I am going to the Father."

John 14:12

Those who hope in the LORD
*   will renew their strength.*
They will soar on wings like eagles;
*   they will run and not grow weary,*
*   they will walk and not be faint.*

Isaiah 40:31

FAITH

Though you have not seen Christ, you love him; and even though you do not see him now, you believe in him and are filled with an inexpressible and glorious joy.

1 Peter 1:8

This is a trustworthy saying that deserves full acceptance (and for this we labor and strive), that we have put our hope in the living God, who is the Savior of all men, and especially of those who believe.

1 Timothy 4:9–10

Jesus said, "I tell you the truth, if you have faith as small as a mustard seed, you can say to this mountain, 'Move from here to there' and it will move. Nothing will be impossible for you."

Matthew 17:20

FAMILY

If you belong to Christ, then you are Abraham's seed, and heirs according to the promise.

Galatians 3:29

Honor your father and your mother, as the LORD your God has commanded you, so that you may live long and that it may go well with you in the land the LORD your God is giving you.

Deuteronomy 5:16

Both the one who makes men holy and those who are made holy are of the same family. So Jesus is not ashamed to call them brothers.

Hebrews 2:11

How great is the love the Father has lavished on us, that we should be called children of God! And that is what we are!

1 John 3:1

FAMILY

God sets the lonely in families.

Psalm 68:6

My people will live in peaceful dwelling places,
*   in secure homes,*
*   in undisturbed places of rest.*

Isaiah 32:18

If a widow has children or grandchildren, these should learn first of all to put their religion into practice by caring for their own family and so repaying their parents and grandparents, for this is pleasing to God.

1 Timothy 5:4

Children's children are a crown to the aged,
*   and parents are the pride of their children.*

Proverbs 17:6

As we have opportunity, let us do good to all people, especially to those who belong to the family of believers.

Galatians 6:10

FELLOWSHIP

Jesus said, "Where two or three come together in my name, there am I with them."

Matthew 18:20

If we walk in the light, as Christ is in the light, we have fellowship with one another.

1 John 1:7

Live in harmony with one another; be sympathetic, love as brothers, be compassionate and humble. Do not repay evil with evil or insult with insult, but with blessing, because to this you were called so that you may inherit a blessing.

1 Peter 3:8–9

In humility consider others better than yourselves. Each of you should look not only to your own interests, but also to the interests of others.

Philippians 2:3–4

FELLOWSHIP

Let us therefore make every effort to do what
leads to peace and to mutual edification.

Romans 14:19

Let the word of Christ dwell in you richly
as you teach and admonish one another
with all wisdom, and as you sing
psalms, hymns and spiritual songs with
gratitude in your hearts to God.

Colossians 3:16

How good and pleasant it is
    when brothers live together in unity!
It is like precious oil poured on the head,
    running down on the beard,
running down on Aaron's beard,
    down upon the collar of his robes.
It is as if the dew of Hermon
    were falling on Mount Zion.
For there the LORD bestows his blessing,
    even life forevermore.

Psalm 133:1-3

FORGIVENESS

If your enemy is hungry, give him food to eat;
*   if he is thirsty, give him water to drink.*
In doing this, you will heap burning coals on
*   his head,*
*   and the L*ORD *will reward you.*

Proverbs 25:21–22

If we confess our sins, he is faithful and just and will forgive us our sins and purify us from all unrighteousness.

1 John 1:9

Blessed is the man
*   whose sin the Lord will never count*
*   against him.*

Romans 4:8

Jesus said, "For if you forgive men when they sin against you, your heavenly Father will also forgive you. But if you do not forgive men their sins, your Father will not forgive your sins."

Matthew 6:14–15

FORGIVENESS

"I, even I, am he who blots out
   your transgressions, for my own sake,
   and remembers your sins no more,"
      declares the LORD.

Isaiah 43:25

As far as the east is from the west,
   so far has he removed our transgressions
      from us.

Psalm 103:12

Bear with each other and forgive whatever grievances you may have against one another. Forgive as the Lord forgave you. And over all these virtues put on love, which binds them all together in perfect unity.

Colossians 3:13–14

If you forgive anyone, I also forgive him. And what I have forgiven—if there was anything to forgive—I have forgiven in the sight of Christ for your sake.

2 Corinthians 2:10

FORGIVENESS

Jesus said, "Forgive, and you will be forgiven."

Luke 6:37

He who covers over an offense promotes love,
but whoever repeats the matter separates
close friends.

Proverbs 17:9

Love covers over all wrongs.

Proverbs 10:12

Peter came to Jesus and asked, "Lord, how many times shall I forgive my brother when he sins against me? Up to seven times?" Jesus answered, "I tell you, not seven times, but seventy-seven times."

Matthew 18:21–22

Blessed is he
whose transgressions are forgiven,
whose sins are covered.
Blessed is the man
whose sin the LORD does not count against him
and in whose spirit is no deceit.

Psalm 32:1–2

FORGIVENESS

You are forgiving and good, O Lord,
  abounding in love to all who call to you.

Psalm 86:5

The law requires that nearly everything
be cleansed with blood, and without the
shedding of blood there is no forgiveness.

Hebrews 9:22

Jesus said, "When you stand praying, if
you hold anything against anyone, forgive him, so that your Father in heaven
may forgive you your sins."

Mark 11:25

A man's wisdom gives him patience;
  it is to his glory to overlook an offense.

Proverbs 19:11

When we were overwhelmed by sins,
  you forgave our transgressions, O Lord.

Psalm 65:3

FRIENDSHIP

Wounds from a friend can be trusted.

Proverbs 27:6

Be devoted to one another in brotherly love. Honor one another above yourselves.

Romans 12:10

A friend loves at all times,
 and a brother is born for adversity.

Proverbs 17:17

Jesus said, "Greater love has no one than this, that he lay down his life for his friends. You are my friends if you do what I command. I no longer call you servants, because a servant does not know his master's business. Instead, I have called you friends, for everything that I learned from my Father I have made known to you."

John 15:13–15

FRIENDSHIP

A man of many companions may come to ruin,
   but there is a friend who sticks closer than a
      brother.

Proverbs 18:24

Do not forsake your friend and
      the friend of your father.

Proverbs 27:10

Two are better than one,
   because they have a good return for their work:
If one falls down,
   his friend can help him up.
But pity the man who falls
   and has no one to help him up!
Also, if two lie down together, they will keep warm.
   But how can one keep warm alone?
Though one may be overpowered,
   two can defend themselves.
A cord of three strands is not quickly broken.

Ecclesiastes 4:9–12

As iron sharpens iron,
   so one man sharpens another.

Proverbs 27:17

GIVING

Jesus said, "Give to everyone who asks you, and if anyone takes what belongs to you, do not demand it back."

Luke 6:30

Each man should give what he has decided in his heart to give, not reluctantly or under compulsion, for God loves a cheerful giver.

2 Corinthians 9:7

Good will come to him who is generous and
lends freely,
who conducts his affairs with justice.

Psalm 112:5

Remember this: Whoever sows sparingly will also reap sparingly, and whoever sows generously will also reap generously.

2 Corinthians 9:6

A generous man will himself be blessed,
for he shares his food with the poor.

Proverbs 22:9

GIVING

I was young and now I am old,
*   yet I have never seen the righteous forsaken*
*   or their children begging bread.*
They are always generous and lend freely;
*   their children will be blessed.*

Psalm 37:25–26

Jesus said, "Give, and it will be given to you. A good measure, pressed down, shaken together and running over, will be poured into your lap. For with the measure you use, it will be measured to you."

Luke 6:38

Jesus said, "When you give to the needy, do not let your left hand know what your right hand is doing, so that your giving may be in secret. Then your Father, who sees what is done in secret, will reward you."

Matthew 6:3–4

GOD'S LOVE

Jesus replied, "He who loves me will be loved by my Father, and I too will love him and show myself to him."

John 14:23

This is how God showed his love among us: He sent his one and only Son into the world that we might live through him. This is love: not that we loved God, but that he loved us and sent his Son as an atoning sacrifice for our sins.

1 John 4:9–10

As high as the heavens are above the earth,
   so great is God's love for those who fear him.

Psalm 103:11

God demonstrates his own love for us in this: While we were still sinners, Christ died for us.

Romans 5:8

GOD'S LOVE

This is how we know what love is: Jesus Christ laid down his life for us. And we ought to lay down our lives for our brothers.

1 John 3:16

From everlasting to everlasting
the LORD's love is with those who fear him,
and his righteousness with their children's
children.

Psalm 103:17

God is love. Whoever lives in love lives in God, and God in him. In this way, love is made complete among us so that we will have confidence on the day of judgment, because in this world we are like him.

1 John 4:16–17

Many are the woes of the wicked,
but the LORD's unfailing love
surrounds the man who trusts in him.

Psalm 32:10

GOD'S WILL

God made known to us the mystery of his will according to his good pleasure, which he purposed in Christ, to be put into effect when the times will have reached their fulfillment—to bring all things in heaven and on earth together under one head, even Christ.

Ephesians 1:9–10

The world and its desires pass away, but the man who does the will of God lives forever.

1 John 2:17

Do not conform any longer to the pattern of this world, but be transformed by the renewing of your mind. Then you will be able to test and approve what God's will is—his good, pleasing and perfect will.

Romans 12:2

GOD'S WILL

In Christ we were also chosen, having been predestined according to the plan of him who works out everything in conformity with the purpose of his will, in order that we, who were the first to hope in Christ, might be for the praise of his glory.

Ephesians 1:11–12

Be joyful always; pray continually; give thanks in all circumstances, for this is God's will for you in Christ Jesus.

1 Thessalonians 5:16–18

Jesus said, "My Father's will is that everyone who looks to the Son and believes in him shall have eternal life, and I will raise him up at the last day."

John 6:40

GOD'S WORD

All Scripture is God-breathed and is useful for teaching, rebuking, correcting and training in righteousness, so that the man of God may be thoroughly equipped for every good work.

2 Timothy 3:16–17

Do not let this Book of the Law depart from your mouth; meditate on it day and night, so that you may be careful to do everything written in it. Then you will be prosperous and successful.

Joshua 1:8

Jesus said, "Heaven and earth will pass away, but my words will never pass away."

Mark 13:31

The word of God is living and active. Sharper than any double-edged sword, it penetrates even to dividing soul and spirit, joints and marrow; it judges the thoughts and attitudes of the heart.

Hebrews 4:12

GOD'S WORD

The man who looks intently into the perfect law that gives freedom, and continues to do this, not forgetting what he has heard, but doing it—he will be blessed in what he does.

James 1:25

Jesus answered, "It is written: 'Man does not live on bread alone, but on every word that comes from the mouth of God.'"

Matthew 4:4

*Your word is a lamp to my feet
and a light for my path.*

Psalm 119:105

*I have hidden your word in my heart
that I might not sin against you.*

Psalm 119:11

Jesus replied, "Blessed are those who hear the word of God and obey it."

Luke 11:28

GRACE

God has saved us and called us to a holy life—not because of anything we have done but because of his own purpose and grace. This grace was given us in Christ Jesus before the beginning of time.

2 Timothy 1:9

God is able to make all grace abound to you, so that in all things at all times, having all that you need, you will abound in every good work.

2 Corinthians 9:8

Because of his great love for us, God, who is rich in mercy, made us alive with Christ even when we were dead in transgressions—it is by grace you have been saved.

Ephesians 2:4-5

The LORD is gracious and compassionate,
slow to anger and rich in love.

Psalm 145:8

GRACE

God gives us more grace. That is why
Scripture says:
> *"God opposes the proud*
> *but gives grace to the humble."*

James 4:6

It is by grace you have been saved,
through faith—and this not from yourselves, it is the gift of God—not by
works, so that no one can boast. For we
are God's workmanship, created in
Christ Jesus to do good works, which
God prepared in advance for us to do.

Ephesians 2:8–10

You know the grace of our Lord Jesus
Christ, that though he was rich, yet for
your sakes he became poor, so that you
through his poverty might become rich.

2 Corinthians 8:9

GRACE

He gives grace to the humble.

Proverbs 3:34

The apostle Paul said, By the grace of God I am what I am, and his grace to me was not without effect. No, I worked harder than all of them—yet not I, but the grace of God that was with me.

1 Corinthians 15:10

It does not, therefore, depend on man's desire or effort, but on God's mercy.

Romans 9:16

God raised us up with Christ and seated us with him in the heavenly realms in Christ Jesus, in order that in the coming ages he might show the incomparable riches of his grace, expressed in his kindness to us in Christ Jesus.

Ephesians 2:6–7

GRACE

He said to me, "My grace is sufficient for you, for my power is made perfect in weakness." Therefore I will boast all the more gladly about my weaknesses, so that Christ's power may rest on me.

2 Corinthians 12:9

Grace and peace be yours in abundance through the knowledge of God and of Jesus our Lord.

2 Peter 1:2

God saved us, not because of righteous things we had done, but because of his mercy. He saved us through the washing of rebirth and renewal by the Holy Spirit, whom he poured out on us generously through Jesus Christ our Savior, so that, having been justified by his grace, we might become heirs having the hope of eternal life.

Titus 3:5-7

HEAVEN

According to the Lord's own word, we tell you that we who are still alive, who are left till the coming of the Lord, will certainly not precede those who have fallen asleep. For the Lord himself will come down from heaven, with a loud command, with the voice of the archangel and with the trumpet call of God, and the dead in Christ will rise first. After that, we who are still alive and are left will be caught up together with them in the clouds to meet the Lord in the air. And so we will be with the Lord forever. Therefore encourage each other with these words.

1 Thessalonians 4:15–18

HEAVEN

Our citizenship is in heaven. And we
eagerly await a Savior from there, the
Lord Jesus Christ.

Philippians 3:20

God will wipe every tear from their eyes.
There will be no more death or mourning
or crying or pain, for the old order of
things has passed away.

Revelation 21:4

Jesus said, "In my Father's house are
many rooms; if it were not so, I would
have told you. I am going there to prepare a place for you."

John 14:2

Blessed are those who wash their robes,
that they may have the right to the tree
of life and may go through the gates into
the city.

Revelation 22:14

HOLINESS

You ought to live holy and godly lives as you look forward to the day of God and speed its coming.

2 Peter 3:11–12

Once you were alienated from God and were enemies in your minds because of your evil behavior. But now he has reconciled you by Christ's physical body through death to present you holy in his sight, without blemish and free from accusation—if you continue in your faith, established and firm, not moved from the hope held out in the gospel.

Colossians 1:21–23

Make every effort to live in peace with all men and to be holy; without holiness no one will see the Lord.

Hebrews 12:14

God chose us in Christ before the creation of the world to be holy and blameless.

Ephesians 1:4

HOLINESS

Since we have these promises, dear friends, let us purify ourselves from everything that contaminates body and spirit, perfecting holiness out of reverence for God.

2 Corinthians 7:1

Just as God who called you is holy, so be holy in all you do; for it is written: "Be holy, because I am holy."

1 Peter 1:15–16

There is no one holy like the LORD;
there is no one besides you;
there is no Rock like our God.

1 Samuel 2:2

God did not call us to be impure, but to live a holy life.

1 Thessalonians 4:7

HOLY SPIRIT

Do not believe every spirit, but test the spirits to see whether they are from God … This is how you can recognize the Spirit of God: Every spirit that acknowledges that Jesus Christ has come in the flesh is from God.

1 John 4:1–2

Jesus said, "I will ask the Father, and he will give you another Counselor to be with you forever—the Spirit of truth. The world cannot accept him, because it neither sees him nor knows him. But you know him, for he lives with you and will be in you."

John 14:16–17

The Lord is the Spirit and where the Spirit of the Lord is, there is freedom.

2 Corinthians 3:17

HOLY SPIRIT

Repent and be baptized, every one of you, in the name of Jesus Christ for the forgiveness of your sins. And you will receive the gift of the Holy Spirit. The promise is for you and your children and for all who are far off—for all whom the Lord our God will call.

Acts 2:38–39

In the same way, the Spirit helps us in our weakness. We do not know what we ought to pray for, but the Spirit himself intercedes for us with groans that words cannot express. And he who searches our hearts knows the mind of the Spirit, because the Spirit intercedes for the saints in accordance with God's will.

Romans 8:26–27

HOSPITALITY

Offer hospitality to one another without grumbling.

1 Peter 4:9

An overseer must be hospitable, one who loves what is good, who is self-controlled, upright, holy and disciplined.

Titus 1:8

Share with God's people who are in need. Practice hospitality.

Romans 12:13

There will always be poor people in the land. Therefore I command you to be openhanded toward your brothers and toward the poor and needy in your land.

Deuteronomy 15:11

Do not forget to entertain strangers, for by so doing some people have entertained angels without knowing it. Remember those in prison as if you were their fellow prisoners, and those who are mistreated as if you yourselves were suffering.

Hebrews 13:2-3

HOSPITALITY

Jesus said, "If anyone gives even a cup of cold water to one of these little ones because he is my disciple, I tell you the truth, he will certainly not lose his reward."

Matthew 10:42

Jesus said, "The King will say to those on his right, 'Come, you who are blessed by my Father; take your inheritance, the kingdom prepared for you since the creation of the world. For I was hungry and you gave me something to eat, I was thirsty and you gave me something to drink, I was a stranger and you invited me in, I needed clothes and you clothed me, I was sick and you looked after me, I was in prison and you came to visit me.'"

Matthew 25:34-36

HUMILITY

By the grace given me I say to every one of you: Do not think of yourself more highly than you ought, but rather think of yourself with sober judgment, in accordance with the measure of faith God has given you.

Romans 12:3

Not that we are competent in ourselves to claim anything for ourselves, but our competence comes from God.

2 Corinthians 3:5

I can do everything through Christ who gives me strength.

Philippians 4:13

The LORD sustains the humble
but casts the wicked to the ground.

Psalm 147:6

Pride goes before destruction,
a haughty spirit before a fall.

Proverbs 16:18

HUMILITY

Your attitude should be the same as that
of Christ Jesus:
Who, being in very nature God,
did not consider equality with God some
thing to be grasped,
but made himself nothing,
taking the very nature of a servant,
being made in human likeness.
And being found in appearance as a man,
he humbled himself
and became obedient to death—even
death on a cross!

Philippians 2:5–8

Clothe yourselves with humility toward
one another, because,
"God opposes the proud
but gives grace to the humble."

1 Peter 5:5

HUMILITY

The fear of the LORD teaches a man wisdom,
and humility comes before honor.

Proverbs 15:33

Humility and the fear of the LORD
bring wealth and honor and life.

Proverbs 22:4

The LORD takes delight in his people;
he crowns the humble with salvation.

Psalm 149:4

The LORD guides the humble in what is right
and teaches them his way.

Psalm 25:9

Jesus said, "The greatest among you will
be your servant. For whoever exalts himself will be humbled, and whoever humbles himself will be exalted."

Matthew 23:11–12

Jesus said, "Whoever humbles himself
like this child is the greatest in the kingdom of heaven."

Matthew 18:4

HUMILITY

When pride comes, then comes disgrace,
but with humility comes wisdom.

Proverbs 11:2

Humble yourselves before the Lord, and
he will lift you up.

James 4:10

Do nothing out of selfish ambition or
vain conceit, but in humility consider
others better than yourselves.

Philippians 2:3

Remind the people to be subject to rulers
and authorities, to be obedient, to be
ready to do whatever is good, to slander
no one, to be peaceable and considerate,
and to show true humility toward all men.

Titus 3:1–2

INTEGRITY

I know, my God, that you test the heart
and are pleased with integrity.

1 Chronicles 29:17

The LORD God is a sun and shield;
    the LORD bestows favor and honor;
no good thing does he withhold
    from those whose walk is blameless.

Psalm 84:11

God holds victory in store for the upright,
    he is a shield to those whose walk is blameless,
for he guards the course of the just
    and protects the way of his faithful ones.

Proverbs 2:7–8

The man of integrity walks securely,
    but he who takes crooked paths will be
        found out.

Proverbs 10:9

INTEGRITY

The integrity of the upright guides them,
but the unfaithful are destroyed by their
duplicity.

Proverbs 11:3

In my integrity you uphold me
and set me in your presence forever.

Psalm 41:12

Those who walk uprightly
enter into peace;
they find rest as they lie in death.

Isaiah 57:2

When a man's ways are pleasing to the LORD,
he makes even his enemies live at peace
with him.

Proverbs 16:7

Someone will say, "You have faith; I have
deeds." Show me your faith without
deeds, and I will show you my faith by
what I do.

James 2:18

JESUS

He will be great and will be called the Son of the Most High. The Lord God will give him the throne of his father David.

Luke 1:32

Therefore the Lord himself will give you a sign: The virgin will be with child and will give birth to a son, and will call him Immanuel.

Isaiah 7:14

When Jesus spoke again to the people, he said, "I am the light of the world. Whoever follows me will never walk in darkness, but will have the light of life."

John 8:12

I am coming soon. Hold on to what you have, so that no one will take your crown.

Revelation 3:11

Our citizenship is in heaven. And we eagerly await a Savior from there, the Lord Jesus Christ.

Philippians 3:20

JESUS

The Spirit of the LORD will rest on him—
*   the Spirit of wisdom and of understanding,*
*   the Spirit of counsel and of power,*
*   the Spirit of knowledge and of the fear*
*   of the LORD.*

Isaiah 11:2

Then Jesus came to them and said, "All authority in heaven and on earth has been given to me. Therefore go and make disciples of all nations, ... teaching them to obey everything I have commanded you. And surely I am with you always, to the very end of the age."

Matthew 28:18–20

When Christ, who is your life, appears, then you also will appear with him in glory.

Colossians 3:4

Be patient and stand firm, because the Lord's coming is near.

James 5:8

JUDGMENT

Speak up for those who cannot speak for
themselves,
for the rights of all who are destitute.
Speak up and judge fairly;
defend the rights of the poor and needy.

Proverbs 31:8-9

Let us stop passing judgment on one another. Instead, make up your mind not to put any stumbling block or obstacle in your brother's way.

Romans 14:13

Speak and act as those who are going to be judged by the law that gives freedom, because judgment without mercy will be shown to anyone who has not been merciful. Mercy triumphs over judgment.

James 2:12-13

JUDGMENT

You ... have no excuse, you who pass judgment on someone else, for at whatever point you judge the other, you are condemning yourself, because you who pass judgment do the same things.

Romans 2:1

This is what the LORD Almighty says: "Administer true justice; show mercy and compassion to one another."

Zechariah 7:9

Do not show partiality in judging; hear both small and great alike. Do not be afraid of any man, for judgment belongs to God.

Deuteronomy 1:17

JUSTIFICATION

Since we have been justified through faith, we have peace with God through our Lord Jesus Christ.

Romans 5:1

God made Jesus who had no sin to be sin for us, so that in him we might become the righteousness of God.

2 Corinthians 5:21

Just as the result of one trespass was condemnation for all men, so also the result of one act of righteousness was justification that brings life for all men. For just as through the disobedience of the one man the many were made sinners, so also through the obedience of the one man the many will be made righteous.

Romans 5:18-19

You see that a person is justified by what he does and not by faith alone.

James 2:24

JUSTIFICATION

The law was put in charge to lead us to
Christ that we might be justified by faith.

Galatians 3:24

You were washed, you were sanctified,
you were justified in the name of the Lord
Jesus Christ and by the Spirit of our God.

1 Corinthians 6:11

God presented Christ as a sacrifice of
atonement, through faith in his blood.
He did this to demonstrate his justice,
because in his forbearance he had left
the sins committed beforehand unpunished—he did it to demonstrate his justice at the present time, so as to be just
and the one who justifies those who
have faith in Jesus.

Romans 3:25–26

KINDNESS

A kindhearted woman gains respect,
  but ruthless men gain only wealth.

Proverbs 11:16

Be kind and compassionate to one another, forgiving each other, just as in Christ God forgave you.

Ephesians 4:32

A kind man benefits himself,
  but a cruel man brings trouble on himself.

Proverbs 11:17

Live in harmony with one another; be sympathetic, love as brothers, be compassionate and humble.

1 Peter 3:8

Make every effort to add to your faith goodness; and to goodness, knowledge; and to knowledge, self-control; and to self-control, perseverance; and to perseverance, godliness; and to godliness, brotherly kindness; and to brotherly kindness, love.

2 Peter 1:5-7

KINDNESS

Jesus said, "In everything, do to others what you would have them do to you, for this sums up the Law and the Prophets."

Matthew 7:12

Whoever is kind to the needy honors God.

Proverbs 14:31

*"With everlasting kindness
I will have compassion on you,"
says the* LORD *your Redeemer.*

Isaiah 54:8

Love is patient, love is kind. It does not envy, it does not boast, it is not proud.

1 Corinthians 13:4

Make sure that nobody pays back wrong for wrong, but always try to be kind to each other and to everyone else.

1 Thessalonians 5:15

LEADERSHIP

Kings detest wrongdoing,
   for a throne is established through
      righteousness.

Proverbs 16:12

Jesus said, "But you are not to be like that. Instead, the greatest among you should be like the youngest, and the one who rules like the one who serves."

Luke 22:26

Love and faithfulness keep a king safe;
   through love his throne is made secure.

Proverbs 20:28

Jesus said, "Leave them; they are blind guides. If a blind man leads a blind man, both will fall into a pit."

Matthew 15:14

By justice a king gives a country stability,
   but one who is greedy for bribes tears it
      down.

Proverbs 29:4

LEADERSHIP

If a king judges the poor with fairness,
*   his throne will always be secure.*

Proverbs 29:14

Be strong and courageous, because you will lead these people to inherit the land I swore to their forefathers to give them.

Joshua 1:6

Therefore, you kings, be wise;
*   be warned, you rulers of the earth.*
Serve the LORD with fear
*   and rejoice with trembling.*

Psalm 2:10–11

We have different gifts, according to the grace given us. If a man's gift . . . is serving, let him serve; if it is teaching, let him teach; if it is encouraging, let him encourage; if it is contributing to the needs of others, let him give generously; if it is leadership, let him govern diligently; if it is showing mercy, let him do it cheerfully.

Romans 12:6–8

LIFE

Jesus declared, "I am the bread of life. He who comes to me will never go hungry, and he who believes in me will never be thirsty."

John 6:35

Set your hearts on things above, where Christ is seated at the right hand of God. Set your minds on things above, not on earthly things. For you died, and your life is now hidden with Christ in God. When Christ, who is your life, appears, then you also will appear with him in glory.

Colossians 3:1-4

Count yourselves dead to sin but alive to God in Christ Jesus.

Romans 6:11

Through Christ Jesus the law of the Spirit of life set me free from the law of sin and death.

Romans 8:2

LIFE

Jesus said, "The Spirit gives life; the flesh counts for nothing. The words I have spoken to you are spirit and they are life."

John 6:63

If the Spirit of him who raised Jesus from the dead is living in you, he who raised Christ from the dead will also give life to your mortal bodies through his Spirit, who lives in you.

Romans 8:11

The Spirit of God has made me;
the breath of the Almighty gives me life.

Job 33:4

You have made known to me the paths of life;
you will fill me with joy in your presence.

Acts 2:28

LOVE

God is love. Whoever lives in love lives in God, and God in him.

1 John 4:16

Dear friends, let us love one another for love comes from God. Everyone who loves has been born of God and knows God.

1 John 4:7

As God's chosen people, holy and dearly loved, clothe yourselves with compassion, kindness, humility, gentleness and patience. Bear with each other and forgive whatever grievances you may have against one another. Forgive as the Lord forgave you. And over all these virtues put on love, which binds them all together in perfect unity.

Colossians 3:12–14

LOVE

You yourselves have been taught by God to love each other.

1 Thessalonians 4:9

These three remain: faith, hope, and love. But the greatest of these is love. Follow the way of love.

1 Corinthians 13:13—14:1

May the Lord make your love increase and overflow for each other and for everyone else.

1 Thessalonians 3:12

The goal is love, which comes from a pure heart and a good conscience and a sincere faith.

1 Timothy 1:5

Love must be sincere. Hate what is evil; cling to what is good. Be devoted to one another in brotherly love.

Romans 12:9

LOVING GOD

Know therefore that the LORD your God is God; he is the faithful God, keeping his covenant of love to a thousand generations of those who love him and keep his commands.

Deuteronomy 7:9

Love the LORD, all his saints!
  The LORD preserves the faithful,
  but the proud he pays back in full.

Psalm 31:23

Delight yourself in the LORD
  and he will give you the desires of your
    heart.

Psalm 37:4

Whom have I in heaven but you?
  And earth has nothing I desire besides you.
My flesh and my heart may fail,
  but God is the strength of my heart
  and my portion forever.

Psalm 73:25—26

LOVING GOD

*"Because he loves me," says the LORD, "I will
rescue him,*
*I will protect him, for he acknowledges
my name."*

Psalm 91:14

The LORD watches over all who love him,
but all the wicked he will destroy.

Psalm 145:20

Jesus replied: "Love the Lord your God
with all your heart and with all your soul
and with all your mind. This is the first
and greatest commandment."

Matthew 22:37–38

We know that in all things God works for
the good of those who love him, who have
been called according to his purpose.

Romans 8:28

The man who loves God is known by God.

1 Corinthians 8:3

MATERIALISM

Honor the LORD with your wealth,
with the firstfruits of all your crops;
then your barns will be filled to overflowing,
and your vats will brim over with new wine.

Proverbs 3:9-10

A good man leaves an inheritance for
his children's children,
but a sinner's wealth is stored up for
the righteous.

Proverbs 13:22

Godliness with contentment is great
gain. For we brought nothing into the
world, and we can take nothing out of it.
But if we have food and clothing, we will
be content with that.

1 Timothy 6:6-8

Jesus answered, "If you want to be perfect, go, sell your possessions and give
to the poor, and you will have treasure in
heaven. Then come, follow me."

Matthew 19:21

MATERIALISM

He who is kind to the poor lends to the LORD,
and he will reward him for what he
has done.

Proverbs 19:17

Moreover, when God gives any man
wealth and possessions, and enables him
to enjoy them, to accept his lot and be
happy in his work—this is a gift of God.

Ecclesiastes 5:19

A generous man will prosper;
he who refreshes others will himself be
refreshed.

Proverbs 11:25

So do not worry, saying, 'What shall we
eat?' or 'What shall we drink?' or 'What
shall we wear?' . . . But seek first his
kingdom and his righteousness, and all
these things will be given to you as well.

Matthew 6:31, 33

MATURITY

It was Christ who gave some to be apostles, some to be prophets, some to be evangelists, and some to be pastors and teachers, to prepare God's people for works of service, so that the body of Christ may be built up until we all reach unity in the faith and in the knowledge of the Son of God and become mature, attaining to the whole measure of the fullness of Christ.

Ephesians 4:11–13

It is God who works in you to will and to act according to his good purpose.

Philippians 2:13

Like newborn babies, crave pure spiritual milk, so that by it you may grow up in your salvation.

1 Peter 2:2

MATURITY

Teach us to number our days aright,
*   that we may gain a heart of wisdom.*

Psalm 90:12

God who began a good work in you will
carry it on to completion until the day of
Christ Jesus.

Philippians 1:6

Let us leave the elementary teachings
about Christ and go on to maturity.

Hebrews 6:1

Instruct a wise man and he will be wiser still;
*   teach a righteous man and he will add to his*
*   learning.*

Proverbs 9:9

Anyone who lives on milk, being still an
infant, is not acquainted with the teaching about righteousness. But solid food is
for the mature, who by constant use
have trained themselves to distinguish
good from evil.

Hebrews 5:13–14

MONEY

A good man leaves an inheritance for
his children's children,
but a sinner's wealth is stored up for
the righteous.

Proverbs 13:22

Jesus said to them, "Watch out! Be on your guard against all kinds of greed; a man's life does not consist in the abundance of his possessions."

Luke 12:15

He who gathers money little by little makes
it grow.

Proverbs 13:11

My God will meet all your needs according to his glorious riches in Christ Jesus.

Philippians 4:19

Keep your lives free from the love of money and be content with what you have, because God has said,

"Never will I leave you;
never will I forsake you."

Hebrews 13:5

MONEY

Jesus said, "Whoever can be trusted with very little can also be trusted with much, and whoever is dishonest with very little will also be dishonest with much."

Luke 16:10

Honor the LORD with your wealth,
with the firstfruits of all your crops;
then your barns will be filled to overflowing,
and your vats will brim over with new wine.

Proverbs 3:9–10

Jesus said, "So do not worry, saying, 'What shall we eat?' or 'What shall we drink?' or 'What shall we wear?' For the pagans run after all these things, and your heavenly Father knows that you need them. But seek first his kingdom and his righteousness, and all these things will be given to you as well."

Matthew 6:31–33

OBEDIENCE

It is not those who hear the law who are righteous in God's sight, but it is those who obey the law who will be declared righteous.

Romans 2:13

Jesus said, "Everyone who hears these words of mine and puts them into practice is like a wise man who built his house on the rock. The rain came down, the streams rose, and the winds blew and beat against that house; yet it did not fall, because it had its foundation on the rock."

Matthew 7:24-25

Jesus said, "Whoever practices and teaches these commands will be called great in the kingdom of heaven."

Matthew 5:19

If anyone obeys his word, God's love is truly made complete in him. This is how we know we are in him.

1 John 2:5

OBEDIENCE

Jesus said, "If you obey my commands, you will remain in my love, just as I have obeyed my Father's commands and remain in his love. I have told you this so that my joy may be in you and that your joy may be complete."

John 15:10–11

It is the LORD your God you must follow, and him you must revere. Keep his commands and obey him; serve him and hold fast to him.

Deuteronomy 13:4

If they obey and serve him,
   they will spend the rest of their days in
      prosperity
   and their years in contentment.

Job 36:11

PATIENCE

I waited patiently for the LORD;
he turned to me and heard my cry.

Psalm 40:1

Be patient, then, brothers, until the Lord's coming. See how the farmer waits for the land to yield its valuable crop and how patient he is for the autumn and spring rains. You too, be patient and stand firm, because the Lord's coming is near.

James 5:7–8

Bear with each other and forgive whatever grievances you may have against one another. Forgive as the Lord forgave you.

Colossians 3:13

A man's wisdom gives him patience;
it is to his glory to overlook an offense.

Proverbs 19:11

A fool shows his annoyance at once,
but a prudent man overlooks an insult.

Proverbs 12:16

PATIENCE

Be joyful in hope, patient in affliction,
faithful in prayer.

Romans 12:12

Be completely humble and gentle; be
patient, bearing with one another in love.

Ephesians 4:2

Warn those who are idle, encourage the
timid, help the weak, be patient with
everyone.

1 Thessalonians 5:14

A patient man has great understanding,
but a quick-tempered man displays folly.

Proverbs 14:29

The end of a matter is better than its beginning,
and patience is better than pride.

Ecclesiastes 7:8

PERSEVERANCE

Blessed is the man who perseveres under trial, because when he has stood the test, he will receive the crown of life that God has promised to those who love him.

James 1:12

The God of all grace, who called you to his eternal glory in Christ, after you have suffered a little while, will himself restore you and make you strong, firm and steadfast.

1 Peter 5:10

Our light and momentary troubles are achieving for us an eternal glory that far outweighs them all.

2 Corinthians 4:17

To those who by persistence in doing good seek glory, honor and immortality, he will give eternal life.

Romans 2:7

PERSEVERANCE

My comfort in my suffering is this:
Your promise preserves my life.

Psalm 119:50

My steps have held to your paths;
my feet have not slipped.

Psalm 17:5

Perseverance must finish its work so that you may be mature and complete, not lacking anything.

James 1:4

Let us not become weary in doing good, for at the proper time we will reap a harvest if we do not give up.

Galatians 6:9

Those who sow in tears
will reap with songs of joy.

Psalm 126:5

All hard work brings a profit,
but mere talk leads only to poverty.

Proverbs 14:23

PRAYER

Jesus said, "Watch and pray so that you will not fall into temptation. The spirit is willing, but the body is weak."

Matthew 26:41

You will call upon me and come and pray to me, and I will listen to you.

Jeremiah 29:12

If my people, who are called by my name, will humble themselves and pray and seek my face and turn from their wicked ways, then will I hear from heaven and will forgive their sin and will heal their land.

2 Chronicles 7:14

What other nation is so great as to have their gods near them the way the Lord our God is near us whenever we pray to him?

Deuteronomy 4:7

PRAYER

Devote yourselves to prayer, being watchful and thankful.

Colossians 4:2

Pray continually.

1 Thessalonians 5:17

The prayer offered in faith will make the sick person well; the Lord will raise him up. If he has sinned, he will be forgiven.

James 5:15

Jesus said, "When you stand praying, if you hold anything against anyone, forgive him, so that your Father in heaven may forgive you your sins."

Mark 11:25

Pray in the Spirit on all occasions with all kinds of prayers and requests. With this in mind, be alert and always keep on praying for all the saints.

Ephesians 6:18

PRIORITIES

Jesus said, "Seek first his kingdom and his righteousness, and all these things will be given to you as well."

Matthew 6:33

Now all has been heard;
here is the conclusion of the matter:
Fear God and keep his commandments,
for this is the whole duty of man.

Ecclesiastes 12:13

We make it our goal to please God, whether we are at home in the body or away from it.

2 Corinthians 5:9

Jesus said, "No one can serve two masters. Either he will hate the one and love the other, or he will be devoted to the one and despise the other. You cannot serve both God and Money."

Matthew 6:24

PRIORITIES

He who pursues righteousness and love
finds life, prosperity and honor.

Proverbs 21:21

Flee the evil desires of youth, and pursue righteousness, faith, love and peace, along with those who call on the Lord out of a pure heart.

2 Timothy 2:22

Like newborn babies, crave pure spiritual milk, so that by it you may grow up in your salvation.

1 Peter 2:2

Forgetting what is behind and straining toward what is ahead, I press on toward the goal to win the prize for which God has called me heavenward in Christ Jesus.

Philippians 3:13-14

Jehoshaphat also said to the king of Israel, "First seek the counsel of the LORD."

1 Kings 22:5

PURPOSE

Do not conform any longer to the pattern of this world, but be transformed by the renewing of your mind. Then you will be able to test and approve what God's will is—his good, pleasing and perfect will.

Romans 12:2

The LORD will fulfill his purpose for me;
your love, O LORD, endures forever—
do not abandon the works of your hands.

Psalm 138:8

We constantly pray for you, that our God may count you worthy of his calling, and that by his power he may fulfill every good purpose of yours and every act prompted by your faith.

2 Thessalonians 1:11

We know that in all things God works for the good of those who love him, who have been called according to his purpose.

Romans 8:28

PURPOSE

We are God's workmanship, created in Christ Jesus to do good works, which God prepared in advance for us to do.

Ephesians 2:10

Because God wanted to make the unchanging nature of his purpose very clear to the heirs of what was promised, he confirmed it with an oath. God did this so that ... we who have fled to take hold of the hope offered to us may be greatly encouraged.

Hebrews 6:17–18

Everyone who confesses the name of the Lord must turn away from wickedness.... If a man cleanses himself from the latter, he will be an instrument for noble purposes, made holy, useful to the Master and prepared to do any good work.

2 Timothy 2:19, 21

REDEMPTION

I have swept away your offenses like a cloud,
your sins like the morning mist.
Return to me,
for I have redeemed you.

Isaiah 44:22

It is because of him that you are in Christ Jesus, who has become for us wisdom from God—that is, our righteousness, holiness and redemption.

1 Corinthians 1:30

In Christ we have redemption through his blood, the forgiveness of sins, in accordance with the riches of God's grace.

Ephesians 1:7

You came near when I called you,
and you said, "Do not fear."
O Lord, you took up my case;
you redeemed my life.

Lamentations 3:57–58

REDEMPTION

You know that it was not with perishable things such as silver or gold that you were redeemed from the empty way of life handed down to you from your forefathers, but with the precious blood of Christ, a lamb without blemish or defect.

1 Peter 1:18-19

All have sinned and fall short of the glory of God, and are justified freely by his grace through the redemption that came by Christ Jesus.

Romans 3:23-24

Put your hope in the LORD,
for with the LORD is unfailing love
and with him is full redemption.

Psalm 130:7

REDEMPTION

Praise the LORD.
He provided redemption for his people;
* he ordained his covenant forever—*
* holy and awesome is his name.*

Psalm 111:1, 9

God redeemed us in order that the blessing given to Abraham might come to the Gentiles through Christ Jesus.

Galatians 3:14

We ourselves, who have the firstfruits of the Spirit, groan inwardly as we wait eagerly for our adoption as sons, the redemption of our bodies.

Romans 8:23

REDEMPTION

Christ redeemed us from the curse of the law by becoming a curse for us, for it is written: "Cursed is everyone who is hung on a tree."

Galatians 3:13

He did not enter by means of the blood of goats and calves; but he entered the Most Holy Place once for all by his own blood, having obtained eternal redemption.

Hebrews 9:12

God has rescued us from the dominion of darkness and brought us into the kingdom of the Son he loves, in whom we have redemption, the forgiveness of sins.

Colossians 1:13–14

RELATIONSHIPS

Be kind and compassionate to one another, forgiving each other, just as in Christ God forgave you.

Ephesians 4:32

Here I am! I stand at the door and knock. If anyone hears my voice and opens the door, I will come in and eat with him, and he with me.

Revelation 3:20

Jesus said, "Whatever you did for one of the least of these brothers of mine, you did for me."

Matthew 25:40

Two are better than one,
*   because they have a good return for their work:*
If one falls down,
*   his friend can help him up.*
But pity the man who falls
*   and has no one to help him up!*

Ecclesiastes 4:9–10

RELATIONSHIPS

Jesus said, "Love your neighbor as yourself."

Matthew 22:39

Jesus said, "All men will know that you are my disciples, if you love one another."

John 13:35

Carry each other's burdens, and in this way you will fulfill the law of Christ. . . . Therefore, as we have opportunity, let us do good to all people, especially to those who belong to the family of believers.

Galatians 6:2, 10

Jesus said, "You have heard that it was said, 'Love your neighbor and hate your enemy.' But I tell you: Love your enemies and pray for those who persecute you, that you may be sons of your Father in heaven."

Matthew 5:43–45

He who walks with the wise grows wise.

Proverbs 13:20

REPENTANCE

Peter replied, "Repent and be baptized, every one of you, in the name of Jesus Christ for the forgiveness of your sins. And you will receive the gift of the Holy Spirit."

Acts 2:38

The Lord is not slow in keeping his promise, as some understand slowness. He is patient with you, not wanting anyone to perish, but everyone to come to repentance.

2 Peter 3:9

If a wicked man turns away from all the sins he has committed and keeps all my decrees and does what is just and right, he will surely live; he will not die.

Ezekiel 18:21

REPENTANCE

Jesus said, "If your brother sins, rebuke him, and if he repents, forgive him. If he sins against you seven times in a day, and seven times comes back to you and says, 'I repent,' forgive him."

Luke 17:3-4

Repent, then, and turn to God, so that your sins may be wiped out, that times of refreshing may come from the Lord.

Acts 3:19

Jesus said, "I tell you that in the same way there will be more rejoicing in heaven over one sinner who repents than over ninety-nine righteous persons who do not need to repent."

Luke 15:7

REPUTATION

Jesus said to his host, "When you give a luncheon or dinner, do not invite your friends, your brothers or relatives, or your rich neighbors; if you do, they may invite you back and so you will be repaid. But when you give a banquet, invite the poor, the crippled, the lame, the blind, and you will be blessed. Although they cannot repay you, you will be repaid at the resurrection of the righteous."

Luke 14:12–14

The nations will see your righteousness,
  and all kings your glory;
you will be called by a new name
  that the mouth of the LORD will bestow.

Isaiah 62:2

REPUTATION

Jesus said, "The greatest among you will be your servant. For whoever exalts himself will be humbled, and whoever humbles himself will be exalted."

Matthew 23:11–12

A good name is more desirable than great riches;
*   to be esteemed is better than silver or gold.*

Proverbs 22:1

An elder must be blameless, the husband of but one wife, a man whose children believe and are not open to the charge of being wild and disobedient. Since an overseer is entrusted with God's work, he must be blameless—not overbearing, not quick-tempered, not given to drunkenness, not violent, not pursuing dishonest gain. Rather he must be hospitable, one who loves what is good, who is self-controlled, upright, holy and disciplined.

Titus 1:6–8

RESPONSIBILITY

And the things you have heard me say in the presence of many witnesses entrust to reliable men who will also be qualified to teach others.

2 Timothy 2:2

The man who plants and the man who waters have one purpose, and each will be rewarded according to his own labor.

1 Corinthians 3:8

Jesus said, "The man who had received the five talents brought the other five. 'Master,' he said, 'you entrusted me with five talents. See, I have gained five more.' His master replied, 'Well done, good and faithful servant! You have been faithful with a few things; I will put you in charge of many things. Come and share your master's happiness!'"

Matthew 25:20—21

RESPONSIBILITY

Suppose there is a righteous man
who does what is just and right....
He follows my decrees
and faithfully keeps my laws.
That man is righteous;
he will surely live,

declares the Sovereign LORD.

Ezekiel 18:5, 9

Jesus said, "You are the light of the world. A city on a hill cannot be hidden. Neither do people light a lamp and put it under a bowl. Instead they put it on its stand, and it gives light to everyone in the house. In the same way, let your light shine before men, that they may see your good deeds and praise your Father in heaven."

Matthew 5:14–16

RIGHTEOUSNESS

Jesus said,
"Blessed are those who hunger and thirst
    for righteousness,
  for they will be filled."

Matthew 5:6

Sow for yourselves righteousness,
  reap the fruit of unfailing love,
and break up your unplowed ground;
  for it is time to seek the LORD,
until he comes
  and showers righteousness on you.

Hosea 10:12

The fruit of righteousness will be peace;
  the effect of righteousness will be quietness
    and confidence forever.

Isaiah 32:17

In the way of righteousness there is life;
  along that path is immortality.

Proverbs 12:28

He who pursues righteousness and love
  finds life, prosperity and honor.

Proverbs 21:21

RIGHTEOUSNESS

Surely he will never be shaken;
a righteous man will be remembered forever.
He will have no fear of bad news;
his heart is steadfast, trusting in the LORD.

Psalm 112:6–7

The mouth of the righteous man utters wisdom,
and his tongue speaks what is just.
The law of his God is in his heart;
his feet do not slip.

Psalm 37:30–31

The eyes of the Lord are on the righteous
and his ears are attentive to their prayer.

1 Peter 3:12

Religion that God our Father accepts as pure
and faultless is this: to look after orphans
and widows in their distress and to keep
oneself from being polluted by the world.

James 1:27

God does not take his eyes off the righteous;
he enthrones them with kings
and exalts them forever.

Job 36:7

SALVATION

God our Savior ... wants all men to be saved and to come to a knowledge of the truth.

1 Timothy 2:3-4

God says,
"*In the time of my favor I heard you,*
     and in the day of salvation I helped you."
I tell you, now is the time of God's favor, now is the day of salvation.

2 Corinthians 6:2

If you confess with your mouth, "Jesus is Lord," and believe in your heart that God raised him from the dead, you will be saved.

Romans 10:9

Once made perfect, Jesus became the source of eternal salvation for all who obey him.

Hebrews 5:9

SALVATION

All the prophets testify about Jesus that everyone who believes in him receives forgiveness of sins through his name.

Acts 10:43

Jesus said, "Whoever believes and is baptized will be saved, but whoever does not believe will be condemned."

Mark 16:16

Jesus saved us, not because of righteous things we had done, but because of his mercy. He saved us through the washing of rebirth and renewal by the Holy Spirit.

Titus 3:5

God did not appoint us to suffer wrath but to receive salvation through our Lord Jesus Christ. He died for us so that, whether we are awake or asleep, we may live together with him.

1 Thessalonians 5:9–10

SELF-CONTROL

The grace of God that brings salvation
has appeared to all men. It teaches us to
say "No" to ungodliness and worldly pas-
sions, and to live self-controlled, upright
and godly lives in this present age.

Titus 2:11–12

The end of all things is near. Therefore
be clear minded and self-controlled so
that you can pray.

1 Peter 4:7

Because Christ himself suffered when he
was tempted, he is able to help those
who are being tempted.

Hebrews 2:18

Let us be self-controlled, putting on faith
and love as a breastplate, and the hope
of salvation as a helmet.

1 Thessalonians 5:8

SELF-CONTROL

Prepare your minds for action; be self-controlled; set your hope fully on the grace to be given you when Jesus Christ is revealed.

1 Peter 1:13

Jesus said to his disciples, "If anyone would come after me, he must deny himself and take up his cross and follow me."

Matthew 16:24

Be self-controlled and alert. Your enemy the devil prowls around like a roaring lion looking for someone to devour.

1 Peter 5:8

If you live according to the sinful nature, you will die; but if by the Spirit you put to death the misdeeds of the body, you will live.

Romans 8:13

SELF-IMAGE

You were taught, with regard to your former way of life, to put off your old self, which is being corrupted by its deceitful desires; to be made new in the attitude of your minds; and to put on the new self, created to be like God in true righteousness and holiness.

Ephesians 4:22–24

Jesus said, "Are not two sparrows sold for a penny? Yet not one of them will fall to the ground apart from the will of your Father. And even the very hairs of your head are all numbered. So don't be afraid; you are worth more than many sparrows."

Matthew 10:29–31

"Before I formed you in the womb I knew you, before you were born I set you apart," says the LORD.

Jeremiah 1:5

SELF-IMAGE

The Spirit himself testifies with our spirit that we are God's children. Now if we are children, then we are heirs—heirs of God and co-heirs with Christ, if indeed we share in his sufferings in order that we may also share in his glory.

Romans 8:16–17

You, O Lord, created my inmost being;
  you knit me together in my mother's womb.
I praise you because I am fearfully and
      wonderfully made;
  your works are wonderful,
  I know that full well.

Psalm 139:13–14

Know that the LORD is God.
  It is he who made us, and we are his;
  we are his people, the sheep of his pasture.

Psalm 100:3

SERVICE

Serve wholeheartedly, as if you were serving the Lord, not men, because you know that the Lord will reward everyone for whatever good he does.

Ephesians 6:7–8

Each one should use whatever gift he has received to serve others, faithfully administering God's grace in its various forms. If anyone speaks, he should do it as one speaking the very words of God. If anyone serves, he should do it with the strength God provides, so that in all things God may be praised through Jesus Christ.

1 Peter 4:10–11

Acknowledge the God of your father, and serve him with wholehearted devotion and with a willing mind, for the LORD searches every heart and understands every motive behind the thoughts.

1 Chronicles 28:9

SERVICE

Whatever you do, work at it with all your heart, as working for the Lord, not for men, since you know that you will receive an inheritance from the Lord as a reward. It is the Lord Christ you are serving.

Colossians 3:23–24

It was Christ who gave some to be apostles, some to be prophets, some to be evangelists, and some to be pastors and teachers, to prepare God's people for works of service, so that the body of Christ may be built up until we all reach unity in the faith and in the knowledge of the Son of God and become mature, attaining to the whole measure of the fullness of Christ.

Ephesians 4:11–13

SIN

Do not let sin reign in your mortal body
so that you obey its evil desires. For sin
shall not be your master, because you
are not under law, but under grace.

Romans 6:12, 14

If we confess our sins, he is faithful and
just and will forgive us our sins and
purify us from all unrighteousness.

1 John 1:9

Just as through the disobedience of the
one man the many were made sinners,
so also through the obedience of the one
man the many will be made righteous.

Romans 5:19

Jesus is the atoning sacrifice for our sins,
and not only for ours but also for the
sins of the whole world.

1 John 2:2

SIN

Jesus said, "In the same way, I tell you, there is rejoicing in the presence of the angels of God over one sinner who repents."

Luke 15:10

If my people, who are called by my name, will humble themselves and pray and seek my face and turn from their wicked ways, then will I hear from heaven and will forgive their sin and will heal their land.

2 Chronicles 7:14

Let the wicked forsake his way
*   and the evil man his thoughts.*
Let him turn to the LORD, and he will have
*   mercy on him,*
*   and to our God, for he will freely pardon.*

Isaiah 55:7

STEWARDSHIP

The Lord answered, "Who then is the faithful and wise manager, whom the master puts in charge of his servants to give them their food allowance at the proper time? It will be good for that servant whom the master finds doing so when he returns."

Luke 12:42–43

Good will come to him who is generous
and lends freely,
who conducts his affairs with justice.

Psalm 112:5

It is required that those who have been given a trust must prove faithful.

1 Corinthians 4:2

Whatever you do, work at it with all your heart, as working for the Lord, not for men, since you know that you will receive an inheritance from the Lord as a reward. It is the Lord Christ you are serving.

Colossians 3:23–24

STEWARDSHIP

"Bring the whole tithe into the store-house, that there may be food in my house. Test me in this," says the LORD Almighty, "and see if I will not throw open the floodgates of heaven and pour out so much blessing that you will not have room enough for it."

Malachi 3:10

Each one should use whatever gift he has received to serve others, faithfully administering God's grace in its various forms. If anyone speaks, he should do it as one speaking the very words of God. If anyone serves, he should do it with the strength God provides, so that in all things God may be praised through Jesus Christ.

1 Peter 4:10–11

STRENGTH

You do not lack any spiritual gift as you eagerly wait for our Lord Jesus Christ to be revealed. He will keep you strong to the end, so that you will be blameless on the day of our Lord Jesus Christ.

1 Corinthians 1:7–8

The LORD gives strength to his people.

Psalm 29:11

I can do everything through Christ who gives me strength.

Philippians 4:13

I kneel before the Father, from whom his whole family in heaven and on earth derives its name. I pray that out of his glorious riches he may strengthen you with power through his Spirit in your inner being.

Ephesians 3:14–16

STRENGTH

Do not fear, for I am with you;
  do not be dismayed, for I am your God.
I will strengthen you and help you;
  I will uphold you with my righteous right hand.

Isaiah 41:10

My flesh and my heart may fail,
  but God is the strength of my heart
  and my portion forever.

Psalm 73:26

God gives strength to the weary
  and increases the power of the weak.

Isaiah 40:29

May the Lord strengthen your hearts so
that you will be blameless and holy in
the presence of our God and Father
when our Lord Jesus comes with all his
holy ones.

1 Thessalonians 3:13

TALENTS AND GIFTS

We have different gifts, according to the grace given us. If a man's gift is prophesying, let him use it in proportion to his faith. If it is serving, let him serve; if it is teaching, let him teach; if it is encouraging, let him encourage; if it is contributing to the needs of others, let him give generously; if it is leadership, let him govern diligently; if it is showing mercy, let him do it cheerfully.

Romans 12:6–8

Every good and perfect gift is from above, coming down from the Father of the heavenly lights, who does not change like shifting shadows.

James 1:17

TALENTS AND GIFTS

God's gifts and his call are irrevocable.

Romans 11:29

Each man has his own gift from God; one has this gift, another has that.

1 Corinthians 7:7

There are different kinds of gifts, but the same Spirit. There are different kinds of service, but the same Lord. There are different kinds of working, but the same God works all of them in all men. Now to each one the manifestation of the Spirit is given for the common good.

1 Corinthians 12:4-7

Each one should use whatever gift he has received to serve others, faithfully administering God's grace in its various forms.

1 Peter 4:10

TEMPTATION

No temptation has seized you except
what is common to man. And God is
faithful; he will not let you be tempted
beyond what you can bear. But when you
are tempted, he will also provide a way
out so that you can stand up under it.

1 Corinthians 10:13

Submit yourselves, then, to God. Resist
the devil, and he will flee from you.

James 4:7

Because Jesus himself suffered when he
was tempted, he is able to help those
who are being tempted.

Hebrews 2:18

Be strong in the Lord and in his mighty
power. Put on the full armor of God so
that you can take your stand against the
devil's schemes.

Ephesians 6:10–11

TEMPTATION

It is for freedom that Christ has set us free. Stand firm, then, and do not let yourselves be burdened again by a yoke of slavery.

Galatians 5:1

Since we have a great high priest who has gone through the heavens, Jesus the Son of God, let us hold firmly to the faith we profess. For we do not have a high priest who is unable to sympathize with our weaknesses, but we have one who has been tempted in every way, just as we are—yet was without sin. Let us then approach the throne of grace with confidence, so that we may receive mercy and find grace to help in our time of need.

Hebrews 4:14–16

THANKFULNESS

Let the word of Christ dwell in you richly
as you teach and admonish one another
with all wisdom, and as you sing
psalms, hymns and spiritual songs with
gratitude in your hearts to God.

Colossians 3:16

Let them give thanks to the LORD for his
*   unfailing love*
* and his wonderful deeds for men,*
for he satisfies the thirsty
*   and fills the hungry with good things.*

Psalm 107:8–9

Just as you received Christ Jesus as Lord,
continue to live in him, rooted and built
up in him, strengthened in the faith as
you were taught, and overflowing with
thankfulness.

Colossians 2:6–7

Give thanks to the LORD, for he is good;
*   his love endures forever.*

1 Chronicles 16:34

THANKFULNESS

You turned my wailing into dancing;
  you removed my sackcloth and clothed me
    with joy,
that my heart may sing to you and not be
    silent.
O LORD my God, I will give you thanks forever.

Psalm 30:11–12

The LORD is my strength and my shield;
  my heart trusts in him, and I am helped.
My heart leaps for joy
  and I will give thanks to him in song.

Psalm 28:7

Since we are receiving a kingdom that
cannot be shaken, let us be thankful,
and so worship God acceptably with reverence and awe.

Hebrews 12:28

Give thanks in all circumstances, for this
is God's will for you in Christ Jesus.

1 Thessalonians 5:18

TRUTH

Kings take pleasure in honest lips;
*   they value a man who speaks the truth.*

Proverbs 16:13

The LORD is near to all who call on him,
*   to all who call on him in truth.*

Psalm 145:18

Jesus answered, "I am the way and the truth and the life. No one comes to the Father except through me."

John 14:6

Joshua said, "I am about to go the way of all the earth. You know with all your heart and soul that not one of all the good promises the LORD your God gave you has failed. Every promise has been fulfilled; not one has failed."

Joshua 23:14

Jesus said, "You will know the truth, and the truth will set you free."

John 8:32

TRUTH

We know also that the Son of God has
come and has given us understanding,
so that we may know him who is true.
And we are in him who is true—even in
his Son Jesus Christ. He is the true God
and eternal life.

1 John 5:20

Buy the truth and do not sell it;
  get wisdom, discipline and understanding.

Proverbs 23:23

Jesus said, "When he, the Spirit of truth,
comes, he will guide you into all truth.
He will not speak on his own; he will
speak only what he hears, and he will
tell you what is yet to come."

John 16:13

All your words are true;
  all your righteous laws are eternal.

Psalm 119:160

WISDOM

The fear of the LORD is the beginning of wisdom;
   all who follow his precepts have good
      understanding.
   To him belongs eternal praise.

                                          Psalm 111:10

Know also that wisdom is sweet to your soul;
   if you find it, there is a future hope for you,
   and your hope will not be cut off.

                                          Proverbs 24:14

Wisdom, like an inheritance, is a good thing
   and benefits those who see the sun.
Wisdom is a shelter
   as money is a shelter,
but the advantage of knowledge is this:
   that wisdom preserves the life of its possessor.

                                          Ecclesiastes 7:11-12

The foolishness of God is wiser than
man's wisdom, and the weakness of God
is stronger than man's strength.

                                          1 Corinthians 1:25

WISDOM

Wisdom is supreme; therefore get wisdom.
Though it cost all you have, get
understanding.

Proverbs 4:7

How much better to get wisdom than gold,
to choose understanding rather than silver!

Proverbs 16:16

Wisdom makes one wise man more powerful
than ten rulers in a city.

Ecclesiastes 7:19

The wisdom that comes from heaven is
first of all pure; then peace-loving, considerate, submissive, full of mercy and
good fruit, impartial and sincere.

James 3:17

Who is like the wise man?
Who knows the explanation of things?
Wisdom brightens a man's face
and changes its hard appearance.

Ecclesiastes 8:1

WORSHIP

Great is the LORD and most worthy of praise;
  he is to be feared above all gods.

1 Chronicles 16:25

Ascribe to the LORD the glory due his name;
  worship the LORD in the splendor of his
    holiness.

Psalm 29:2

I will sing to the LORD,
  for he is highly exalted.
The horse and its rider
  he has hurled into the sea.
The LORD is my strength and my song;
  he has become my salvation.
He is my God, and I will praise him,
  my father's God, and I will exalt him.

Exodus 15:1–2

Come, let us bow down in worship,
  let us kneel before the LORD our Maker.

Psalm 95:6

WORSHIP

Worship the LORD with gladness;
come before him with joyful songs.

Psalm 100:2

Since we are receiving a kingdom that cannot be shaken, let us be thankful, and so worship God acceptably with reverence and awe.

Hebrews 12:28

Jesus said, "A time is coming and has now come when the true worshipers will worship the Father in spirit and truth, for they are the kind of worshipers the Father seeks. God is spirit, and his worshipers must worship in spirit and in truth."

John 4:23–24

For you who revere my name, the sun of righteousness will rise with healing in its wings. And you will go out and leap like calves released from the stall.

Malachi 4:2

At Inspirio we love to hear from you—
your stories, your feedback,
and your product ideas.
Please send your comments to us
by way of e-mail at
icares@zondervan.com
or to the address below:

inspirio™

Attn: Inspirio Cares
5300 Patterson Avenue SE
Grand Rapids, MI 49530

If you would like further information
about Inspirio and the products we create,
please visit us at:
www.inspiriogifts.com

Thank you and God bless!